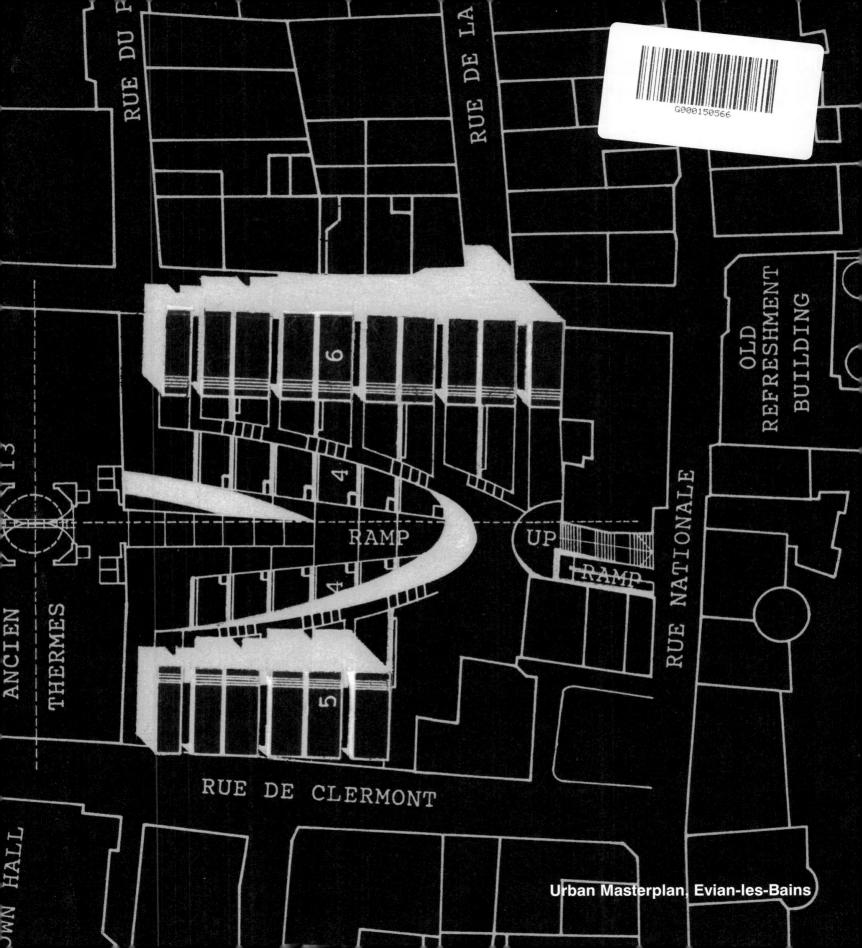

Urban Masterplan, Evian-les-Bains

Hi Robert,

your Dad told me you were thinking
of becoming an architect. I had the
same thoughts when I was your age
and managed to get there.

This is some of my work and I hope
you enjoy looking through, ...follow your dreams...

all the best

28.6.17

studio downie architects

NeoArchitecture

studio downie architects

images
Publishing

Published in Australia in 2006 by
The Images Publishing Group Pty Ltd
ABN 89 059 734 431
6 Bastow Place, Mulgrave, Victoria 3170, Australia
Tel: +61 3 9561 5544 Fax: +61 3 9561 4860
books@images.com.au
www.imagespublishing.com

National Library of Australia Cataloguing-in-Publication entry:

Studio Downie Architects.

Bibliography.
ISBN 1 86470 155 2.
ISBN 978 1 86470 155 5.

1. Downie, Craig. 2. Studio Downie Architects (Firm).
3. Architectural firms – Great Britain – History.
4. Architecture, Modern – 20th century. 5. Architecture, Modern – 21st century.
I. Studio Downie Architects (Firm).
(Series: Neo Architecture).

720.92

Coordinating editor: Robyn Beaver

Design concept by Studio Downie Architects
www.studiodownie.com

Production by The Graphic Image Studio Pty Ltd, Mulgrave, Australia
www.tgis.com.au

Digital production by Splitting Image Colour Studio Pty Ltd, Australia

Printed by Everbest Printing Co. Ltd., in Hong Kong/China

IMAGES has included on its website a page for special notices in relation to this and our other publications.
Please visit www.imagespublishing.com

Contents

Acknowledgments

To Eileen and Lin

Since 1994 a number of people have supported, introduced or commissioned us, and written about or displayed our work at key points during the practice's development. I wish to thank them for their support: in the early years, Laura Downie, Victor Shanley and Wilfred and Jeannette Cass, Gerson Rottenberg, Simon Hodgkinson and Dr Phil Blackburn, Professor Dennis Sharp, Conway Lloyd Morgan, John Welsh, Victoria Thornton, Marcus Field, Naomi Stungo, Catherine Slessor, Janet Turner and Lorna Wain.

In the later years, John McNaughton, Dr Fred Ratcliffe, Professor Peter Carolin and Sir Philip Dowson, Mark Cass, Isobel Allen, Philip Dodd, Hugh Pearman, Agnes Stevenson, Andrew Meade, André Gibbs and Dr Rita Gardner for her huge leap of faith. A special thanks to David Hanna and Christopher Binsted for their dedication to our projects.

The following staff have played an important part in our office: David Andre, Robert Atkinson, Tim Beecher, Matthew Brookes, James Chin, Paul Davison, Laura Downie, Stephen Fisher, Anthony Gill, Gian Givanni, Christopher Harrison, Motoaki Ichijo, Andrew Jackson, David MacDonald, Grahame Middleton, Arita Patel, Zareen Rahman and Krystene Vickers.

The majority of our work has been elegantly recorded by three photographers – Peter Cook, Chris Gascoigne and James Morris – my thanks to them. Thanks also to Morley von Sternberg, Peter McKinven and Katsuhisa Kida.

For their invaluable guidance in producing this book, thanks must go to Alessina Brooks and Robyn Beaver at The Images Publishing Group, to Catherine Slessor, for her considered essay on our work and to Christopher Binsted, who has worked tirelessly with me to bring this to fruition.

Craig Downie
June 2006

Preface

Craig Downie established Studio Downie Architects in London in 1993. The studio's first building, a gallery for the Cass Sculpture Foundation in West Sussex, was completed in 1994. Just over 10 years later, a larger Foundation Centre was completed for the same client. This book examines the work of the studio over the intervening period.

The projects are presented chronologically, in three sections: the first is a series of pavilions and interior interventions, the second contains larger refurbishments and the third features new buildings in the context of historical townscapes and sensitive landscape sites.

In 1994, Craig Downie was invited to speak, along with Toyo Ito, Aldo van Eyck, Ralph Erskine, Giancarlo de Carlo and Eric Parry, at the annual conference of the Royal Incorporation of Architects in Scotland. With no buildings yet completed, he presented three pavilions set in sensitive landscapes: a lakeside retreat in California, a meditation retreat in Hertfordshire and the gallery in West Sussex. Only the last of these was realised but collectively they informed the early design aspirations, moulded by a fusion of experiences, that had influenced Craig Downie.

The natural environment was a primary influence, as were an interest in surfing and the beauty of ocean waves, in particular the Pacific coast of North America; the delicate layering of space, sunlight, shadow and landscape of Japanese temples and gardens; the elegant and transparent designs of Craig Ellwood; and the powerful weaving of new forms into woodland settings by Aalto and Asplund. Consequently, for the three pavilions, a dialogue with and concealment into the landscape became important. Placed close to trees and water, compositions of simple elements become a changing screen for the moving patterns of shadow and sunlight projected within the enclosing landscape.

This early period also confirmed the importance of the 'small project'. When chosen for two larger commissions, the £10-million Parker Library project for Corpus Christi College, Cambridge and the £7.5-million study centre for the Royal Geographical Society (IBG), London, the £125,000 pavilion for the Cass Sculpture Foundation was the firm's only completed building,

These larger projects, together with current commissions for the Lyme Regis Museum and a King's Cross Central building constitute a group of commissions with particularly challenging briefs in historical urban settings.

Again the engagement is with the context, a borrowing of the ingrained and familiar and the weaving of the existing into the new. A garden wall, a terrace or a sea wall are extended and moulded to envelop and inform the new.

Studio Downie's recent building, the Foundation Centre for the Cass Sculpture Foundation, returns to a woodland setting. The themes of contextual balance and integration are evident but the trapezoidal form and the dark grey façade with its musical composition of vertical elements represents a subtle and gradual shift for the direction of the practice, which it will continue to pursue.

Introduction

Craig Downie's first independent project of substance was a primitive hut. For an inaugural project it was an appropriate and auspicious beginning, exploring the notion of the hut in the forest, the archetypal 'first building' that connects with the primitive origins of architecture. Yet in the way it synthesised sophisticated contemporary influences (Mies, Carlo Scarpa, the Californian Case Study House programme), it was far from primitive.

Set deep in an idyllic bluebell woodland in East Sussex, Downie's hut/pavilion provides exhibition and educational spaces for the Hat Hill Sculpture Foundation. His clients were visionary arts patrons Wilfred and Jeannette Cass, and the Foundation is a forum for their remarkable collection of British sculpture. Established masters such as Caro, Frink and Hepworth rub shoulders with younger *arrivistes* and works are dispersed on a changing basis around the woodland grounds of Hat Hill Copse. Completed in 1994, Downie's pavilion is a vital fixed point on the circuit, enlivening the serious business of information and education with visual and tactile delight.

At heart, Downie could be perhaps described as a kind of romantic pragmatist. His approach to architecture is highly poetic in its desire to transcend the everyday, yet this lyricism is underscored by a profound, questing concern for how things are made and put together. It is a persuasive combination. Quoted in an article in *The Guardian*, Wilfred Cass recalls how he selected Downie for the commission. 'All these high powered architects took notes and asked lots of questions. Craig didn't ask anything. His head was down and he was drawing trees and things the whole time. We thought he hadn't listened to any of the brief, but when he came back with his drawings you could see that he totally understood the whole concept.'

Hat Hill marked the flowering of a youthful architectural talent that has since sustained and built on its early promise. Often young architects are beguiled by ambition and the lure of large jobs, precipitating the rapid expansion of their practices; in the rush to conquer the world, they often end up losing their way and their souls. Both in his choice of projects and the manner of their execution, Craig Downie has managed to retain a clear sense of identity that resonates throughout a succession of commissions from a diversity of clients. Since he set up Studio Downie in 1993, these have included tough-minded government bodies, historic institutions, commercial developers and private individuals.

From his time as an architectural student at the Duncan of Jordanstone Art College in Dundee, Downie's career has been tempered and underscored by an intriguing medley of influences. Dundee is a city on Scotland's east coast, steeped in the grit and graft of industry; Downie found intellectual stimulus in the environs of the city's art college. This brought him into contact with sculptors, designers and artists, a creative dynamic he still assiduously cultivates. Along with the work of the incomparable James Stirling, early influences were EM Schumacher's *Small is Beautiful*, and Jane Jacobs' *The Death and Life of Great American Cities*, polemics that stressed the need to cherish the small, the nuanced and the particular above the rapacious *anomie* of globalisation.

After college, like many talented Scots, Downie headed for London where he worked for Terry Farrell on the Clifton Nurseries greenhouse, a tensile structure that stirred a passion for engineering. A spell in the offices of Norman Foster followed and then he went on the road, with periods in California and Australia while making intermittent pilgrimages to explore and assimilate the work of inspirational architects. In Europe it was Aalto, Asplund, Siza and Scarpa; in Japan, Tadao Ando, and in America, Neutra, Ellwood and Kahn.

The influence of the Californian Modernists is particularly apparent in an early unbuilt project for a lakeside house in California. For many young architects the single family dwelling is a familiar testing ground for ideas and here Downie proposed a lightweight pavilion hung from a timber deck, the entire structure supported by soaring steel mast. The concern to impinge as lightly as possible on the surroundings reflects Downie's philosophy of environmental awareness, while the dramatically expressed structure and the cultivation of the house as a setting for the sybaritic pleasures of swimming, boating and sunbathing allude to the elegant, technical economy of Californian Modernism and its associated lifestyles of healthy hedonism.

Downie has also proved adept at adding to and reinvigorating old buildings, devising contextual yet identifiably modern elements that sensitively unite the historic and the contemporary. Projects such as the new library, archives and visitor gallery for the Parker Library at Corpus Christi College in Cambridge and an extension to the Lyme Regis Museum in Dorset engage in a tactful rapport with existing historic structures.

Downie's extension to the Royal Geographical Society in London is a particular tour de force, tipping its hat to the Society's distinguished past, yet also gently blowing the dust off a venerable Victorian institution. The new parts house a reading room and exhibition space, which are treated in very different ways. The exhibition space is a lightweight pavilion floating along the edge of Exhibition Road marking a new public entrance; by contrast the reading room is dug into the courtyard garden and is a virtually imperceptible bunkered, subterranean presence. The relationship between a new glazed volume, Victorian brick buildings and garden quad irresistibly recalls Ahrends Burton and Koralek's extension to Keble College, but here a lush flowering vine is trained around the glazing to create a light and heat-diffusing green screen which merges the building more intimately with the landscape.

Fuelled by a personal interest in abstract sculpture and installation art, Downie's interiors projects are another significant strand of development. His work for the Training and Enterprise Council made the most of modest budgets and created a series of lively interior fit-outs, drawing inspiration from artists such as Donald Judd and Richard Serra in the use of sculptural objects to divide and define space. His coolly judged refurbishment of the Institute of Contemporary Arts reinforces its subterranean, club-like ambience, but also freshens up the interior through the calculated use of colour.

The next phase of Downie's career promises much. He will have a chance to test his ambitions in the gritty setting of London's King's Cross with a mixed use 'gateway' building that forms part of a major urban redevelopment. And with the recent completion of a new Foundation Centre for his loyal patrons Wilfred and Jeanette Cass, Downie has also returned to Hat Hill. Designed to house the Foundation's library and archive, the building is another sophisticated primitive hut, wrapped in an appropriately arboreal skin of vertical cedar fins. There are overtones of Aalto and Japan, but the pervading impression is of an architect who is now secure in himself, calmly relishing the maturing of his talent. The trajectory that Craig Downie began in a bluebell wood more than a decade earlier has come satisfyingly full circle.

Catherine Slessor, Managing Editor, *The Architectural Review*, London

projects

Gallery and Visitors' Pavilion, Cass Sculpture Foundation
The Goodwood Estate, West Sussex

The vision of Wilfred and Jeannette Cass was to create a landscape where British sculptors could realise ambitious works that, without their financial assistance and enthusiastic backing, might never be realised.

The site is within a designated area of Outstanding Natural Beauty – a beautiful 20-acre copse on the South Downs of the Goodwood Estate. Victor Shanley was responsible for the landscape design and the brief was to provide a gallery and visitors' pavilion as a focus for arrival and information, placed centrally in a section of commercial woodland.

The building slides into the rows of trees, the walls a continuation of the lines of trunks, the spaces between maximising cathedral-like, ivy covered vistas.

The sensitive collage of landscape and sculptures exercised a restraint and simplicity to avoid an overly sculptural form. It is a composition of closed and open space; approaching through the landscape there is a deliberate solidity with the dramatic views that are concealed until entry. There is a sense of the landscape passing through, with the long solid walls a backdrop for the trees and the changing pattern of sunlight and shadows they project upon the setting.

The strongest influences are the designs of Craig Ellwood in California and the correlation felt between his work and the temples and gardens visited across Japan. However, the long glass cubes separating the side walls and roof reflect Scarpa's rooflights at his marvellous gallery in Possagno.

Along the east–west axis the elements shift, creating a diagonally symmetrical plan with reflected solid and open planes separated by a large central rooflight that collects sunlight within the tall trees. The north–south axis is a steel goal post that passes out over the side walls with sloping steel purlins projecting in each direction, similar to the rowing skull pattern structure of the Lakeside Retreat. Inside, sculptures and drawings are displayed, lectures are given and visitors use the electronic classroom to gain access to sculptors' portfolios.

The colours and materials are soft and restrained, chosen to merge over time into the ambience of the landscape. A vivid green copper wall is one splash of flamboyance; a reference to arrival, to the surrounding sculptures and contrasting with the subdued, almost white, Finnish pine panels: a beacon in the centre of this most magical place.

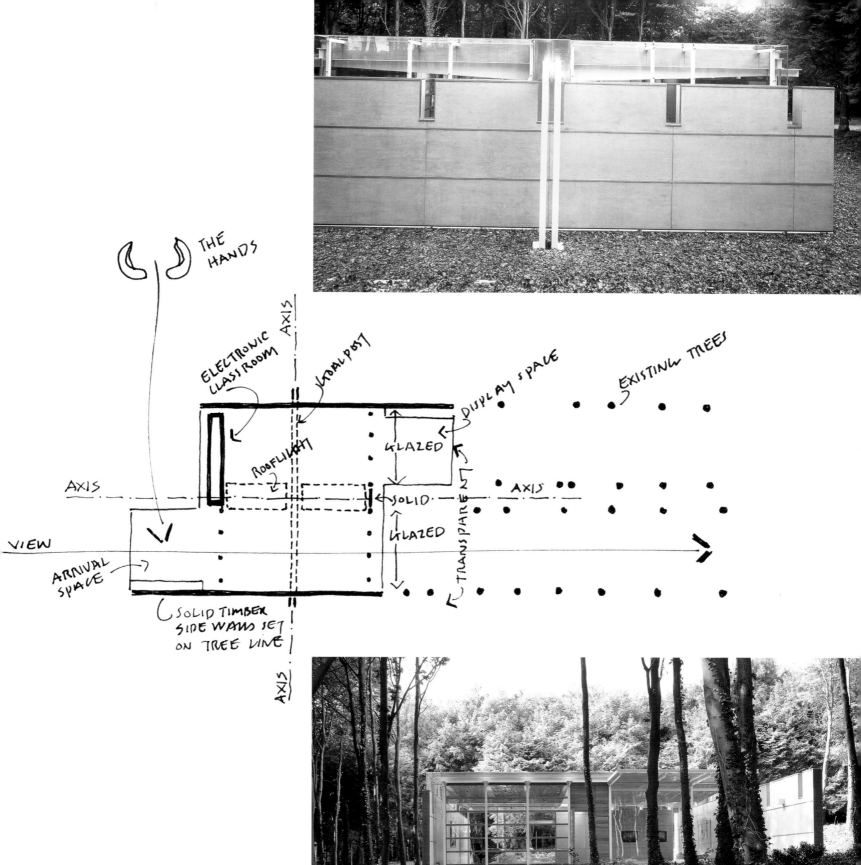

THE HANDS

ELECTRONIC CLASSROOM

GOALPOST

DISPLAY SPACE

EXISTING TREES

ROOFLIGHT

GLAZED

AXIS

SOLID

GLAZED

TRANSPARENT

AXIS

VIEW

ARRIVAL SPACE

SOLID TIMBER SIDE WALLS SET ON TREE LINE

AXIS

AXIS

Lakeside Retreat
California

Escape from the rigours of daily life and a closeness to water were the priorities for this project. Approaching through the forest, a timber quay is set level with the bank. Tall, slim columns placed within the trees support a steel structure based on a rowing scull, with shallow beams creating a sleek, transparent elevation. The living spaces are hidden below, in a glass box suspended over the lake, animated by the shimmering sunlight patterns reflected from the water. Furnishing is minimal, with deckchairs to the living space; the bedrooms are sized for a double futon and a rucksack, avoiding internal clutter and allowing clear views through. All spaces open out to a continuous balcony, where the sound and movement of the water enhance a place for retreat.

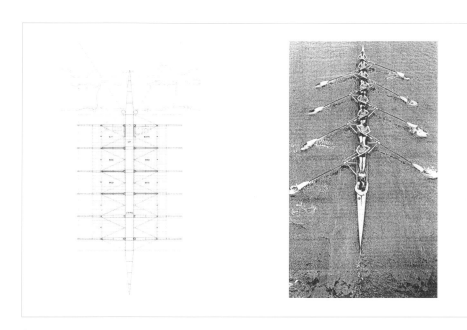

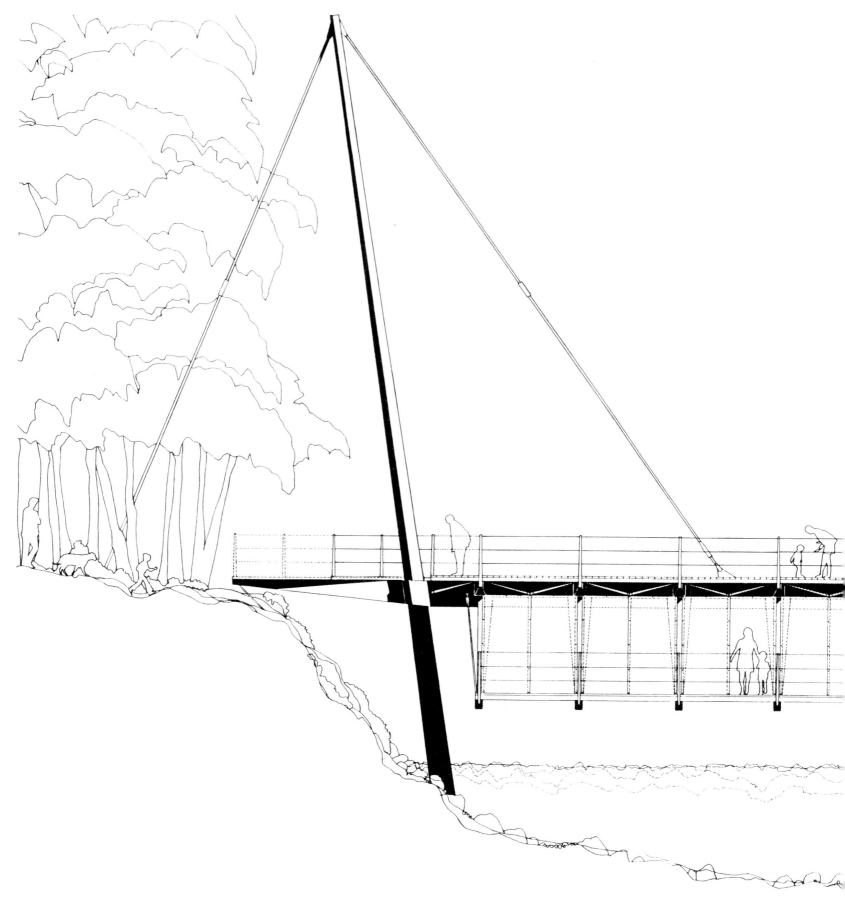

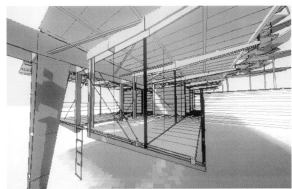

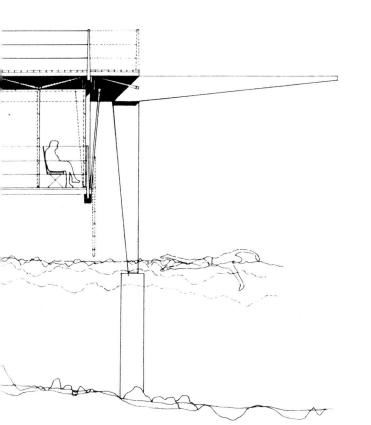

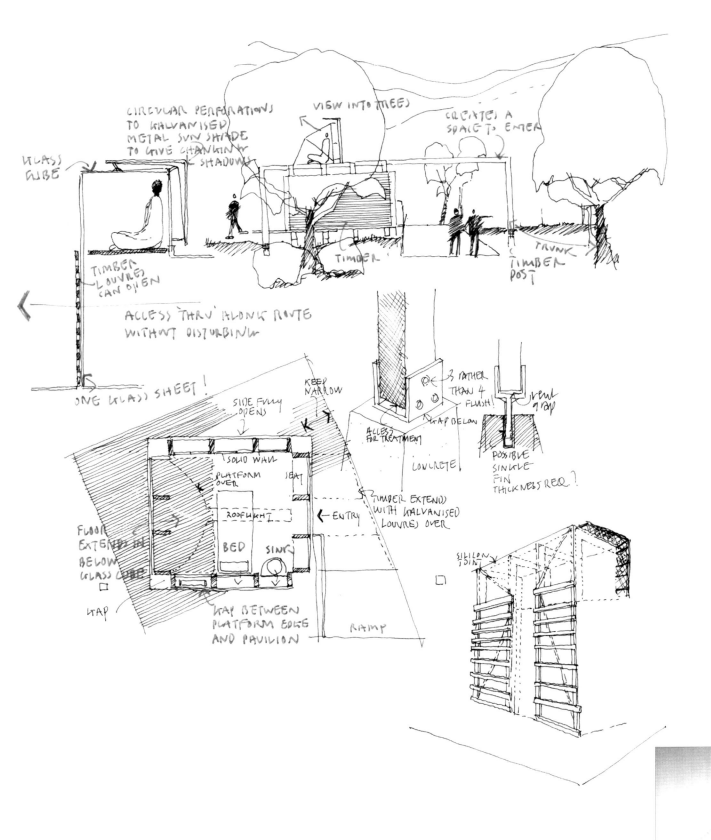

CIRCULAR PERFORATIONS
TO GALVANISED
METAL SUN SHADE
TO GIVE CHANGING
SHADOWS

VIEW INTO TREES

CREATES A
SPACE TO ENTER

GLASS
CUBE

TIMBER
LOUVRES
CAN OPEN

TIMBER

TRUNK
TIMBER
POST

ACCESS THRU' ALONG ROUTE
WITHOUT DISTURBING

ONE GLASS SHEET!

KEEP
NARROW

SIDE FULLY
OPENS

3 RATHER
THAN 4
FLUSH!

GAP BELOW

ACCESS
FOR TREATMENT

CONCRETE

REAL
GAP

SOLID WALL

PLATFORM
OVER

SEAT

ROOFLIGHT

BED

SINK

FLOOR
EXTENDS
BELOW
GLASS CUBE

TIMBER EXTENDS
WITH GALVANISED
LOUVRES OVER

POSSIBLE
SINGLE
FIN
THICKNESS REQ?

ENTRY

GAP
TAP

GAP BETWEEN
PLATFORM EDGE
AND PAVILION

RAMP

SILICON
JOIN

Meditation Retreat for a Recording Studio
Wymondley, Hertfordshire

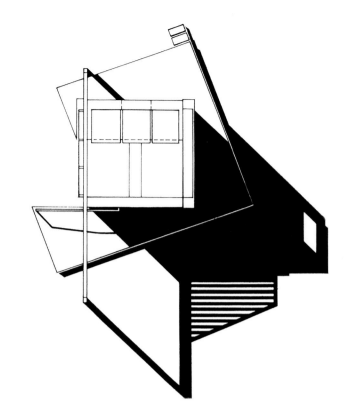

A meditation retreat is carefully placed within a sensitive 14th-century priory landscape with a tithe barn, moat and grove of French box trees. The design includes a processional route of paths, vistas and views including a new timber bridge, several ponds with sculptures and places to sit along the route.

The pavilion is located at the end of a rising vista but positioned off the axis, concealed within and close to the box trees. Only a simple timber post, beam and ramp are seen at the top of the rise.

A glass wall allows views of the trees from within the pavilion, capturing the movement of light and shadows through the branches; at night it acts as a beacon. A bed, washbasin and ladder are concealed in one wall, the latter providing access to a high-level platform where one can sit among the trees. The platform around the pavilion is reduced at points to encourage considered movement at a place of privacy and contemplation.

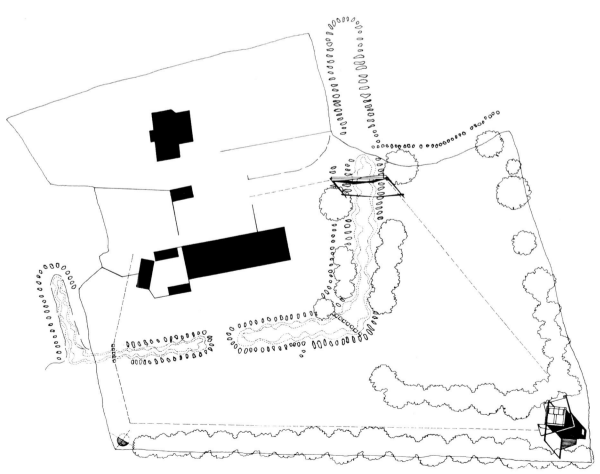

House Refurbishment and Extension
Halesworth, Suffolk

The refurbishment of the Grade II-listed 14th-century long house involves a large and minimal attic bath space, separate living pavilion and a 20-metre lap pool set in protected Suffolk farmland. Field patterns and lines influence the placing of the new forms within the open and flat landscape – the living pavilion is built upon the footprint of an old outhouse, and the pool house is enclosed by a new traditional kitchen garden brick wall and lean-to structure.

There is a continuation of approaches developed through the earlier retreat and pavilion projects. The open and closed relationships with surrounding landscapes are defined by interlocking but separate elements such as goalposts, floating roofs, linear structural grids and the play between glazed and solid façades. Here, the pavilion structure is an oak frame resting on a solid concrete wall, with glazed sliding panels opening on three sides: to the central grassed courtyard and at each end to create a pathway through from the old house down to a stream. The pool house is also defined by solid and transparent façades again opening to the courtyard with the pool water level with the grass.

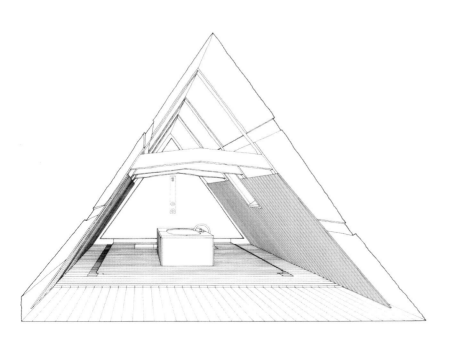

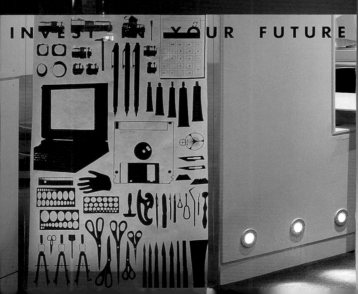

N E X T

T E P

NEXT S T E P

INVEST YOUR FUTURE

125

TELEPHONE 081 896 1010
CAREERS
TRAINING
EDUCATION
OPPORTUNITIES
C.V.S & APPLICATIONS
INTERVIEWS
ADVICE
FOR ADULTS
INDIVIDUALS
PROFESSIONAL
FREEFONE 0800 55 56

P U S H

N

IN

Guidance, training and business development centres, West London TEC

Dr Phil Blackburn, the Chief Executive of the West London Training & Enterprise Council (TEC), proposed a network of one-stop quality advice centres across West London, to address skill shortages and provide career guidance for local residents. Design, and a High Street location close to the post office and chemist were high on the agenda.

With limited budgets and floor plates, investigations addressed the insertion of a single dominant and dramatic form into the spaces to singularly resolve the subtle operational and spatial separation required – public (foyer reception welcome); semi-public (information libraries, meeting); private (interviews, office spaces) – the stages through which visitors are carefully taken.

Key to the design was maximising open transparent space with carefully sculptured elements, creating the necessary privacy and security and avoiding enclosed corridors for a single central space. Drawing on influences by the work of several artists, in particular Richard Serra, Donald Judd and Ben Nicholson, various forms were experimented with: a single curve for Acton and Hounslow, and a series of cubes and layers for Park Royal and Hayes. Themes were a single, strong, but warm and uplifting colour; integrated specially designed furniture; large graphics, with special designs by Malcolm Frost; and top-lit fabric ceilings, emphasising enclosure, softness and focus. At Acton, where the concept was tested, visitors feel they are in a tent, bringing calm and concentration.

In 1995 the project won the national DBA (Design Business Association) Design Effectiveness Award for office/commercial interiors.

Next Step Guidance and Training Centre
Acton Town, London

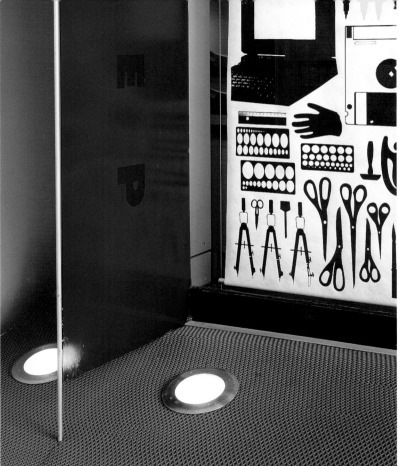

Business Link for Business Development
Hounslow, West London

Next Step Guidance and Training Centre
Hayes, West London

Business Development Centre
Park Royal Partnership
West London

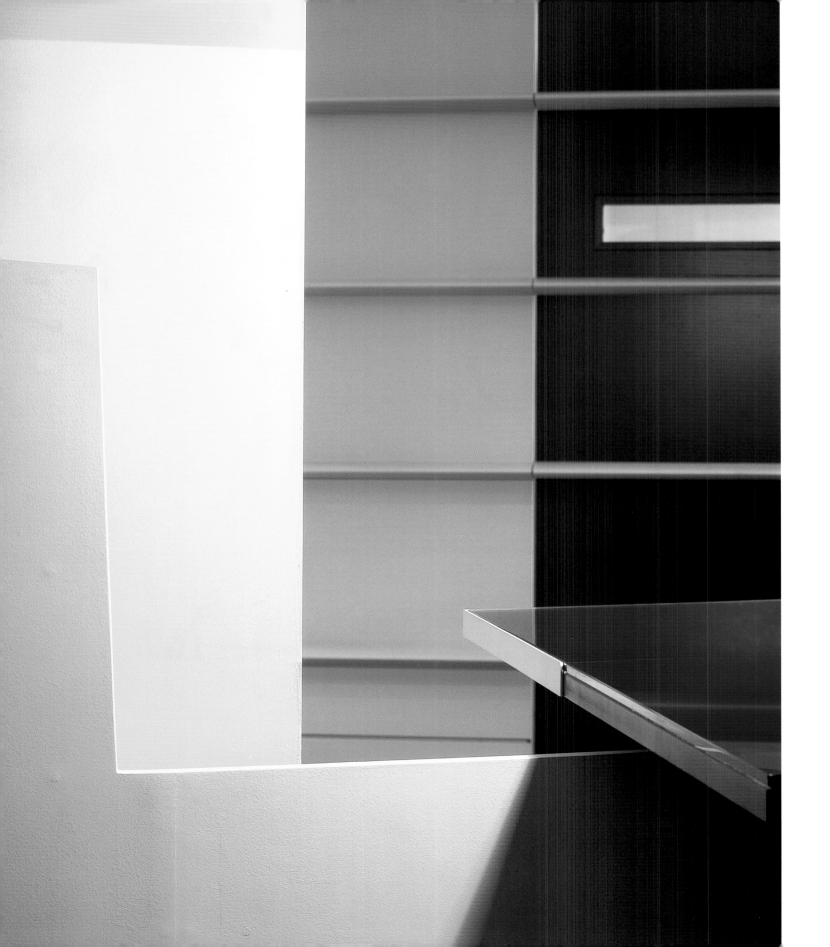

UK Headquarters for CDC Investment Management
The Caisse des Dépôts Group
Piccadilly, London

CDC International Management is a commercial division of the Caisses de Dépôts, the French Treasury. With a network of offices in Tokyo, New York, Frankfurt and Paris, it required an image upgrade and space planning of its London base to create a marketing centre for its products.

A single curve is inserted to create the division of uses with a top-lit fabric ceiling defining the reception and an inner space. Within this, three blue elements represent the arrival, waiting and meeting functions and the curve is sculpted with stepping planes and interlocking elements reflecting the flat sculptural relief studies of Ben Nicholson. Cutting across the curve, horizontal aerofoil shapes form a minimal glass conference room screen. Again, yellow dominates but as a series of layered shades with surrounding deep grey walls bringing a corporate gravitas.

Selected projects and competitions 1992–1999

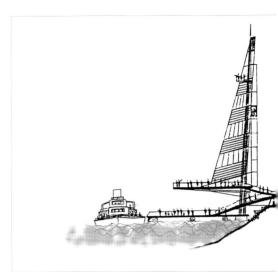

Town Masterplan, Evian-les-Bains

City Square Landmark, Osaka

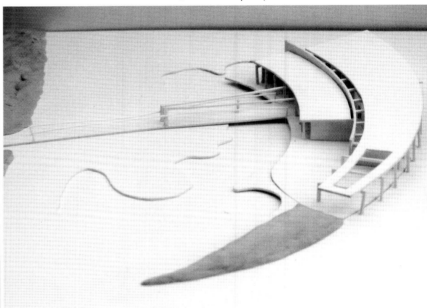

Visitor Centre, Essex

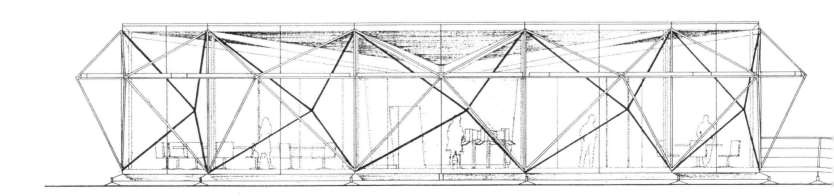

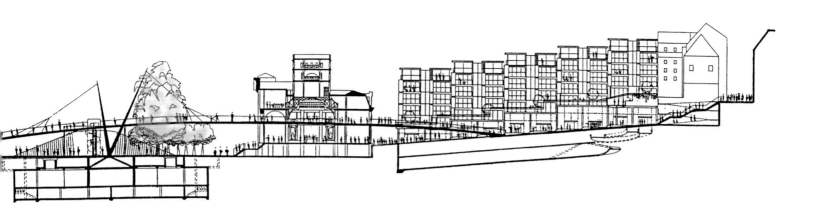

Gallery, Beuvron-en-Auge

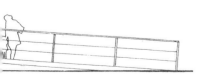

Opportunities Centre, London

Community Opportunities Centre, West London TEC
Southall Town Hall, West London

At the heart of Southall's thriving West London Indian community, a 19th-century town hall had become a vacant and faded Victorian landmark. Proposals for an Opportunities Centre were the catalyst for centralised community services and the transformation of the building to create an inclusive, welcoming public hub. The existing warren-like corridors of heavy dark woods are cleared to create a large open-plan public space with a 25-metre interactive wall integrating reception, library, toilet and interview facilities. Other new sculpted elements are also stitched into the historic fabric to emphasise key points such as the entrance, main stair and information access. From the new transparent sliding doors a single colour theme of yellow threads its way through the spaces, becoming darker as it extends into the building. Set against clear lacquered MDF, American white oak ceiling panels and a central glowing fabric ceiling, the aim is a humane environment on a limited budget.

Office Headquarters Building, BAA-Lynton

St. James' Square, London

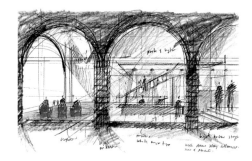

Juxtaposed between a fine London square and Pall Mall, in the heartland of the city's traditional clubs, the brief for a vacant 15,000-square-foot listed building was to develop a marketable product.

An economical, restrained palette of colour and materials was chosen to reflect both the contemporary and traditional nature of the project. Rich wood panels and a plaster ceiling are sculpted to create a minimal reception space set over a deep black slate floor. The theme of wood extends through the building as a focus to each floor, forming the front of the lift cores and the flush washroom panelling. Elsewhere, soft white gives powerful clarity to the existing traditional detailing and a simple background for coloured artwork by Zoe Chamberlain.

Executive Studio for IT Development, West London TEC

Hounslow, West London

The Executive Studio provides training to increase the effectiveness of IT knowledge and improve business performance and is also used for management 'away days' with clients including ICI, BT, Arthur Andersen and Dell. The context was the ordinary interior of a 1980's office building, transformed by creating an inner skin within the retained existing fabric.

The accepted perception of both an office and learning environment is challenged by the design. The spaces consist of the arrival, the paperless office, the studio, the electronic classroom and the 21st-century boardroom. All doors are automatic, sliding glass walls open up to maximise flexibility and there are no traditional desk layouts, resulting in an openness that encourages clear thinking.

Strong graphics and glass divisions create an infinite transparency, a layering of colour, reflection and space and a computerised lighting system allows a variety of moods and periodic colour changes to be set. On arrival a digital picture registers clients and their images are transferred to monitors in the boardroom table, which are set below a dramatic circular glass strip. A central ceiling console opens on four sides to project data onto each wall of the square room; the 20 users respond to questions and the integrated AV provides immediate results.

Film Viewing Suite, Film Library and Offices, The Image Bank
Fitzroy Square, London

The acquisition of an archive of 15,000 American films required the space planning and refurbishment of several office floors to create an integrated suite for film viewing. The director, Mark Cass, also highlighted the need to improve departmental links across existing floor plates and a redundant courtyard was identified as the possible catalyst for change.

A tall skeletal steel structure with four legs and a glazed roof is placed in the courtyard with four arms supporting the glass, set at 45 degrees to the legs. The frame appears poised in space like a helicopter rotor blade, forming a strong visual and operational hub.

Isolated floors and spaces are unified and circulation is improved through this new meeting and breakout area, which opens to a bamboo garden slot. A glass block floor and a spiral stair provide direct access between the film library and the new white, star-shaped viewing suites, against a cool blue background. The lightweight structure is elegant and fragile, minimising impact but maximising the changing sunlight and shadows. At dusk a neon blue strip glows behind the opaque glass panels over the garden.

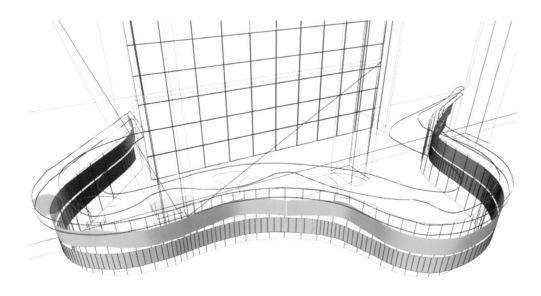

Gallery, Media Centre and Restaurant
Institute of Contemporary Arts (ICA)
The Mall, London

Located on the Mall, the ICA could be seen as quite incongruous, reflecting a bustling, miniature London Soho street rather than the historic environs of St James' Park. A central concourse spine links a variety of entertainments with a bar, restaurant, bookshop, new media centre, cinema, theatre and galleries and a magnet for clubbers with its successful Disco Club nights.

The director, Philip Dodd, wished to increase the sense of welcome and improve wayfinding and 'access for all' while retaining the club ambience within the Grade 1-listed buildings. With limited Arts Council funds, a series of specific enhancements were integrated into the fabric of the interiors, focusing on the central spine.

The largest of these enhancements is the arrival desk, a single sinuous white form floating above a dark grey terrazzo floor. Its woven fascia grows out from the existing walls, weaving and directing visitors. Other elements include a long red couch, new lights, furniture, strong colours identifying specific spaces and a new colour-coded illuminated signage system designed by Milk.

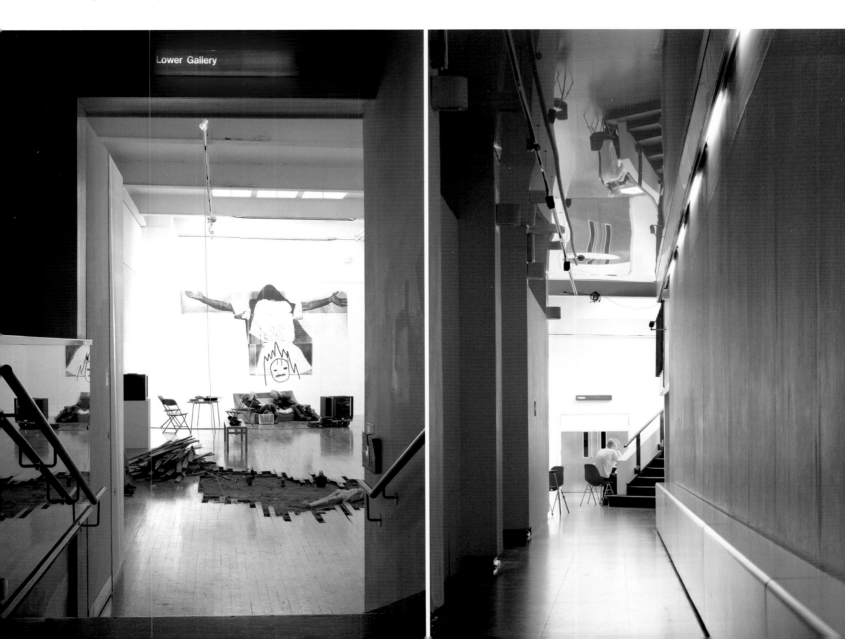

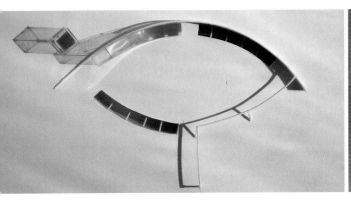

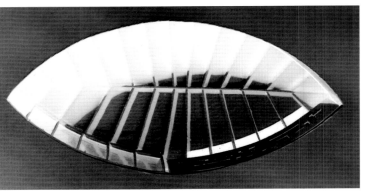

Archive, Maquette Gallery and Offices, Cass Sculpture Foundation

The Goodwood Estate, West Sussex

A second, but unbuilt, project for the Cass Sculpture Foundation is located in a sensitive and exposed south-facing glade sloping down to open farmland. Earlier fluid designs developed into a more refined expression of a natural element: a fallen leaf resting in the landscape. A grass-covered concrete structure, the underside is sculpted with leaf-like veins and encloses an underground maquette gallery cut into the slope with views across the farmland. Approaching through the copse, the concealed space is defined by a curved concrete wall and a glass stair and lift enclosures emerging through the ground into the landscape.

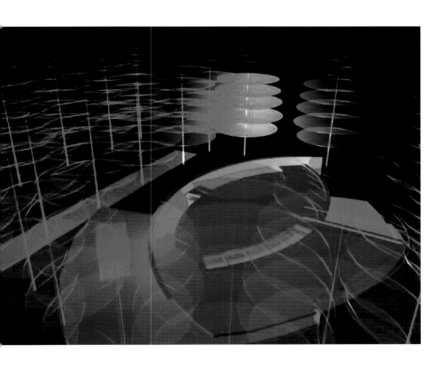

Pool House
Binderton, West Sussex

In open farmland on the West Sussex downs, a former tennis court of nearby Binderton House is approached through a steep copse. Enclosed by thick trees and hedges, it is a surprising manicured setting among the fields. The pool and new pavilion are placed in the far corner of the site, interlocking at the acute angle of tree lines, informing the oblique shape. An open-plan interior is enclosed on three sides with a necklace of wood and glass panels giving intermittent views to the wall of enclosing leafy foliage. The fourth façade is fully glazed with the large sliding doors opening to the expanse of lawn and directly onto the swimming pool. Internally, a ribbon of box wood meanders through the space, across ceilings and walls, evolving into bookcases, study desks and bedside tables.

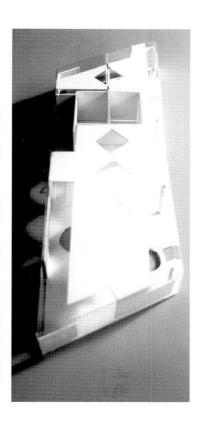

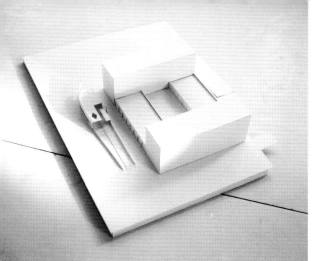

Florence Nightingale Museum, London

Mews Houses, London

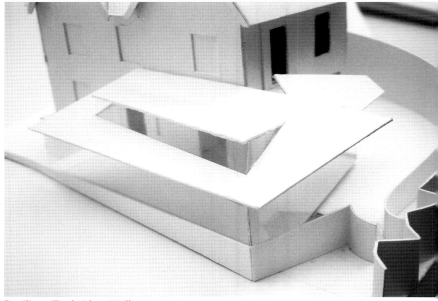

Pavilion, Tunbridge Wells

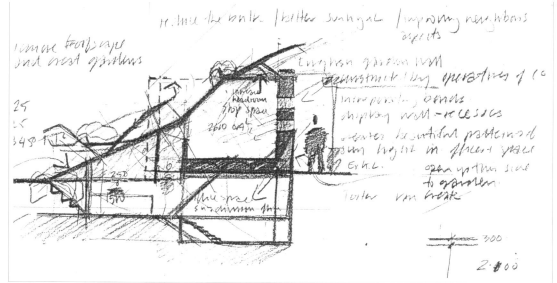

Garden Centre, London

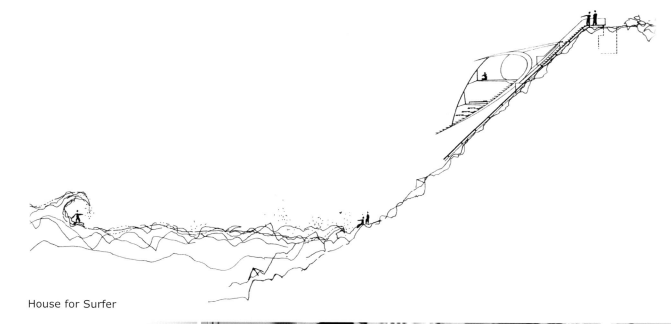

House for Surfer

Community Centre, Croydon

Brick House, London

Ondaatje Theatre, Royal Geographical Society (IBG)

Exhibition Road, London

The historical Grade II-listed theatre completed in 1930 to designs by Kennedy and Nightingale has hosted speakers from Sir Edmund Hillary to Buzz Aldrin. The theatre is a valuable resource for the Royal Geographical Society – refurbishment of the interior was essential to replace the original 750 seats, audio-visual, lighting and mechanical systems – a new contemporary and technological layer would reflect the future of the Society.

The existing space was quite cavernous, without focus or a sense of arrival. The aim was to create a stronger spatial hierarchy, while avoiding major remodelling, to give the sense of a smaller theatre within the larger theatre. Focus is given to the stage, stalls and ceiling to soften the space and create this inner entity. The former faceted lines of the seating and stage are now attractive curves. Interlocking planes of colour accentuate the large screen and above, a large dramatic white sail appears to swoop down towards the stage and is a surface for reflected light. Set against the new deep blue ceiling with its star-like array of lighting, the sweeping white curves and patterns of shadows create an intimacy and counterpoint to the rigid lines, providing a dramatic arrival and focus for the theatre.

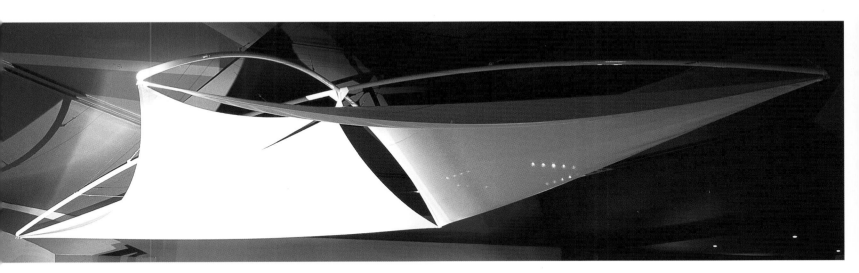

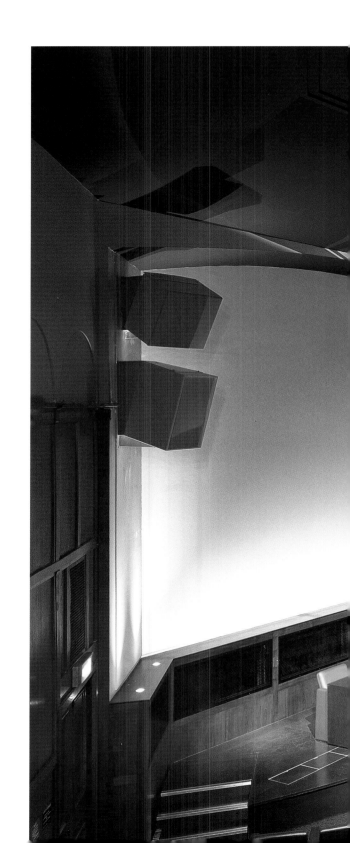

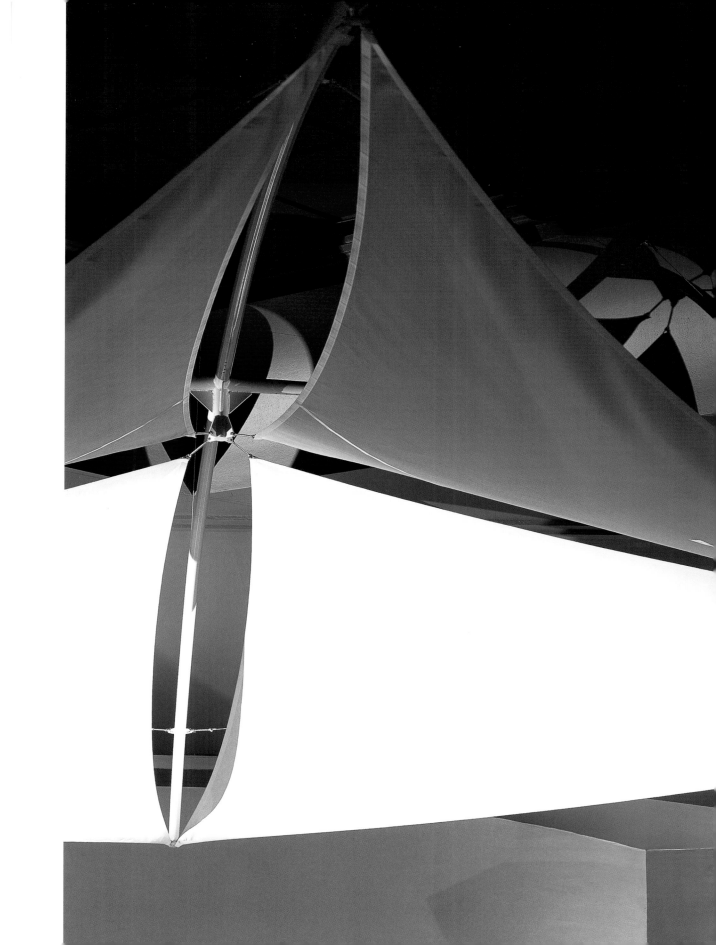

Study Centre: Exhibition, Library, Archive and Education Centre
Royal Geographical Society (IBG)
Exhibition Road, London

For many important societies transformations are often necessary. For the Royal Geographical Society and its director, Dr Rita Gardner, the limitations imposed by its historical Grade II headquarters upon its internationally renowned collection was the catalyst for change. Key to this was to ensure the long-term protection of the two million items in the collection, to increase access for all and change the exclusive perception of the Society with an exciting, transparent and inclusive contemporary public face – *'Unlocking The Archives'*.

New facilities include a reading room, BS 5454 archive storage, an education centre and a new entrance and exhibition pavilion on Exhibition Road. A masterplan was required and, as for Corpus Christi College in Cambridge, this project provided a multi-layered contextual challenge; the historic heritage of Norman Shaw's Lowther Lodge in a landlocked and limited city-centre site with a sensitive and valued, but secret, garden. Retaining the garden setting was key to the concept, achieved by integrating and enhancing existing features.

The long garden terrace in front of Lowther Lodge is rebuilt, widened and extended down Exhibition Road; the reading room and archives are placed underneath, creating a podium for the new pavilion. The pavilion's form and setting is informed by the consideration of two important contextual lines. The first links previously unconnected domains – the secret garden and the public street. The pavilion's concrete canopy, supported on thin circular columns, slopes up towards Exhibition Road. Below, free-standing brick planes and transparent display panels are set perpendicular to the street, allowing an uninterrupted line of vision and inviting engagement with the exhibitions and garden. The spirit of the secret place is continued through acid-etched images on the glass balustrade by the artist Eleanor Long.

The second axis is defined by the pavilion's sculpted pattern of diagonal concrete ceiling beams, which run parallel to the street and extend into the 'Telescope' arrival space. The 'Telescope' stretches from Exhibition Road, through to the garden terrace, framing a new dramatic view of the Royal Albert Hall and the garden elevation of Lowther Lodge. From the 'Telescope' a helical stair passes through the terrace to the reading room and archives, providing dramatic views of Shaw's chimney stacks. The noise level subsides in the quiet calmness of the naturally ventilated reading room where one suddenly feels part of the garden. Long strips of glazing allow views over the garden, sheltered by an arched sunscreen of flowering planting, creating a green natural edge and soft dappled light.

Library, Archives and Visitors' Exhibition Space
Corpus Christi College, Cambridge

For the internationally important Parker Library collection of 20,000 rare manuscripts, books and silver, the college required a new archive, reading room, and visitor exhibition space to ensure the long-term protection of the collection.

The first of several sensitive townscape projects, it initiated studies for integrating the contemporary and traditional, borrowing from the engrained and familiar. The landlocked segment of historical Cambridge presented a sensitive contextual challenge: a Grade I-listed setting designed by William Wilkins, an ancient churchyard and the precious walled Master's garden.

The fine garden wall is the source of inspiration, extended parallel to the church wall as a continuation of the existing traditional English brick detailing. The proposed spaces are stacked vertically within this new narrow strip to maximise protection of the collection and minimise area loss to the Master's garden. Long, contemporary and minimal glass strips are set within the brick wall, providing garden views from the top-lit reading room. A black steel and glass box forms a transition to the Wilkins buildings; with a pergola and new landscaping, the planting is encouraged to grow over and blend the new wall into the garden.

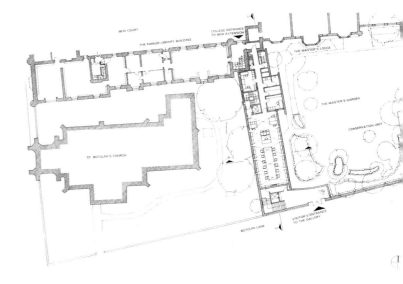

Library and Study Centre
Royal College of Surgeons of England
Lincoln Inns Field, London

This fine Charles Barry Grade II-listed library had a tired interior; careful layering was necessary to integrate new technology with sensitive classical detailing. Dramatic concealed feature lighting, contemporary furniture, new vivid flooring and sympathetic interior colours are combined to strengthen the inherent rhythm and proportional qualities of the space. All existing bookshelves are replaced and a new ventilation and lighting system concealed within the existing fabric. Space planning maximises user capacity and layout flexibility, improving circulation and security control for the library.

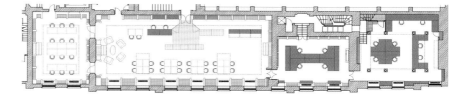

Mixed Use Gateway Building, Argent Estates Ltd
King's Cross Central, London

A Victorian enclave forms the gateway to London's largest urban masterplan. Centred between King's Cross and St. Pancras Station is a collection of small passages, squares and historic buildings, including the German Gymnasium and the Stanley Building. With a fabric of strong rhythms, brickwork piers and robust detailing, a new building investigates the integration of the traditional and the contemporary – the Stanley and a new 50,000-square-foot mixed-use extension.

The response within the sensitive townscape is to ease the transition of scale and materials from the existing to the wider masterplan. Façades and forms respond to surrounding squares, passageways, streetscapes and larger neighbours, creating a gateway to a transitional square. The existing passageway network is extended to form a tall entrance lightwell and separation between new and existing. The new is higher, a deliberate clear hierarchy that steps in scale up to the neighbouring buildings by David Chipperfield Architects, Porphyrios Architects and Caruso St. John. Visually robust, but wafer thin, brick pilasters define each corner; anchors for a protruding grid of black horizontals and tall, elegant silver fins.

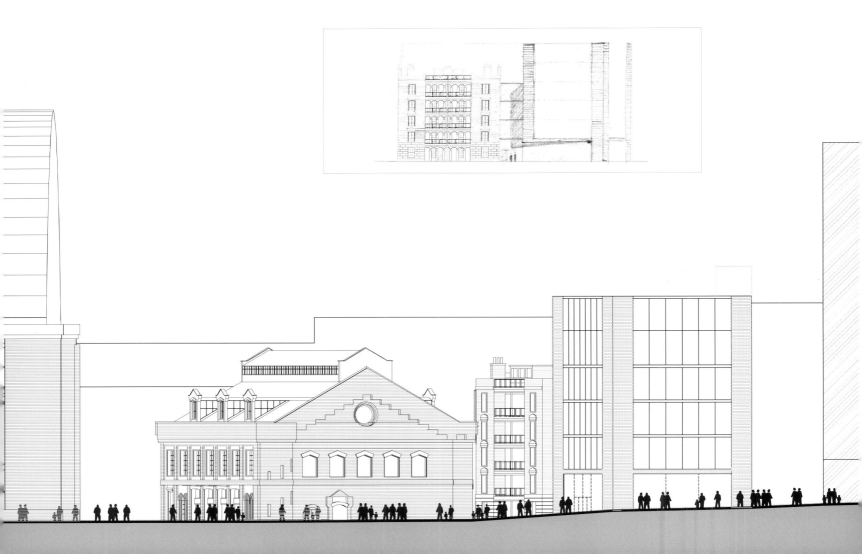

Archives, Gallery and Education Centre
Philpot Lyme Regis Museum, Dorset

A wonderful ocean location, a contextually interesting jumble of render, stone and roofscapes that tumble along the Jurassic coast. The famous Cobb, the old stone sea wall, a fine listed existing museum in a townscape of changing levels and intricate passageways, are components of this sensitive world heritage site. The familiar and accepted is borrowed to extend and weave into the new. The old sea wall is taken up, breaking like a wave across the existing terrain. Creating a new element in the townscape, it rises away from the existing museum, retaining the visibility and integrity of its fine ocean façade. Set between are secondary stepped overlapping layers of white rendered new space and roof terraces. The town's pattern of passageways also threads over and through the new education and gallery spaces, emerging as a minimal glass box that cantilevers out through the sea wall towards the Cobb and ocean views.

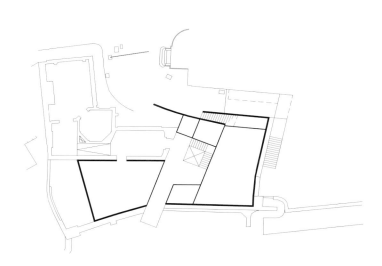

Foundation Centre: Gallery, Library and Archives, Cass Sculpture Foundation
The Goodwood Estate, West Sussex

The Cass Sculpture Foundation was the location of Studio Downie's first completed project in 1994. In 2004, a new building was required for its unique and rapidly growing 21st-century British sculpture archive and library and Studio Downie was appointed to design the Foundation Centre. Inspiration would again be drawn from the beautiful sylvan setting of the copse, but with a larger building required there was a new challenge to weave into the existing.

Responding to lines in the landscape, a trapezoidal form is cut low into the slope of a small valley. A green sedum roof creates an extension of the surrounding grass slopes; concrete fingers extending out and into the chalk slopes encourages new planting to grow over and conceal the rear of the building within the landscape. This lower element, with offices, stores and archives also conceals, enveloping the largest new volume, a 7-metre-high display and seminar space that partly protrudes though the sedum roof. Flat façades of textured render in two shades of grey form simple backdrops, capturing the landscape's theatre of changing patterns of light and shadows. From these hang an array of rough wood fins, reflecting and blending with the enclosing trees. The composition of the fins is a response to the spirit of the place, an interpretation of the rhythms for Debussy's score *Prélude a l'après-midi d'un faune*, also a world of beautiful secret glades in a woodland setting.

The front entrance façade faces a beautiful slope of ivy and tall trees. A long simple elevation, it is punctuated with two windows. The first is the corner entrance space with an oblique view through the depth of the building to the rear chalk slope. The second much larger window is the display space, divided into four panels with the lower two opening to link the landscape and the interior. The display space is defined by a tall white concrete ribbed table placed separately within a blockwork and concrete enclosure. North-facing rooflights set in the deep concrete ribs control sunlight, forming a pattern of glowing light across the ceiling. Unlike the homogeneity of Studio Downie's earlier wood-clad visitor gallery where boundaries are blurred between the inside and out into the landscape, here there is a clear and more deliberate separation. The shades of grey and white are a reference to the local flint but also contribute to a juxtaposition between the built and natural form. The interior robustness and restraint contrast with the soft and vibrant landscape, with the timber fins providing the transition between building and copse.

**Gallery and Visitors' Pavilion,
Cass Sculpture Foundation**

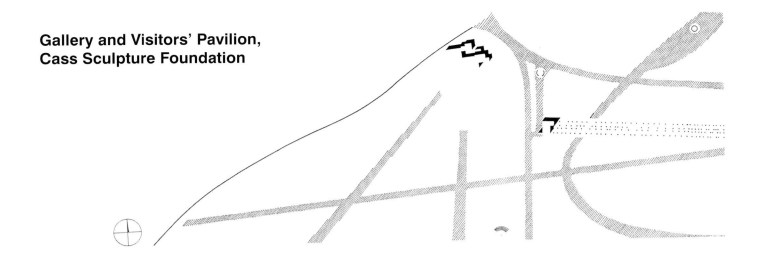

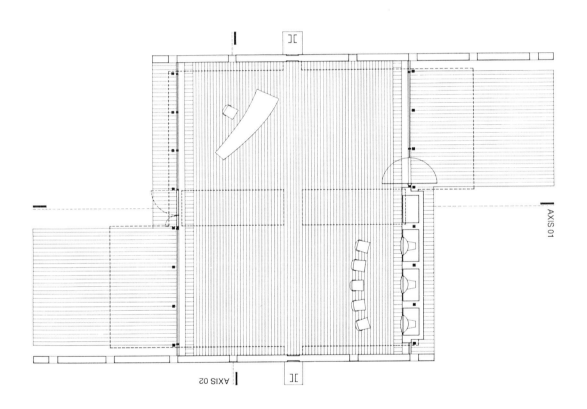

AXIS 01

AXIS 02

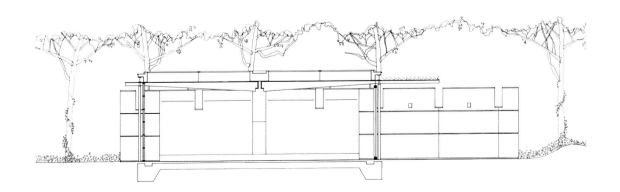

Foundation Centre: Gallery, Library and Archives, Cass Sculpture Foundation

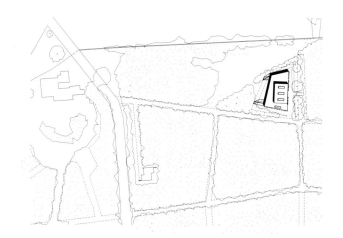

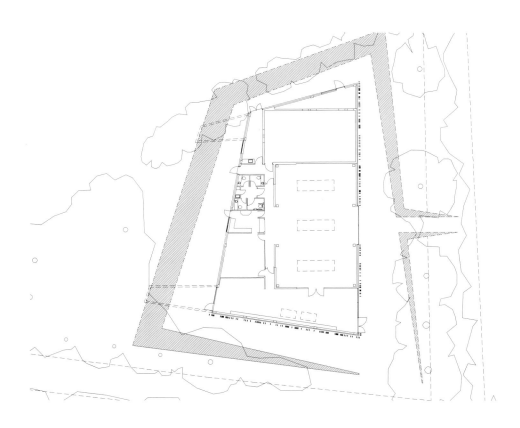

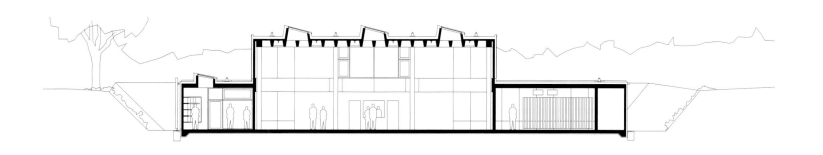

**Study Centre:
Exhibition, Library,
Archive and
Education Centre,
Royal Geographical
Society (IBG)**

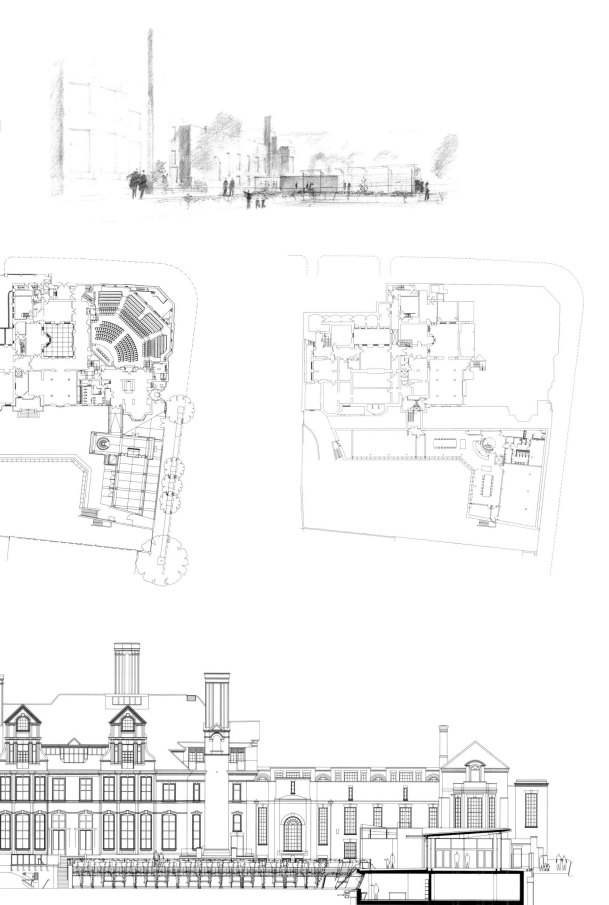

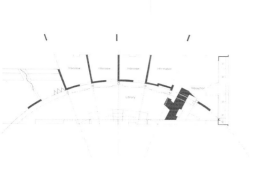

Next Step Guidance and Training Centre, Acton Town

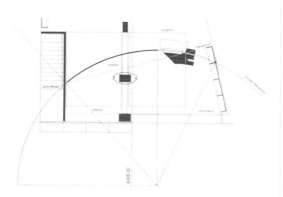

Business Link for Business Development, Hounslow

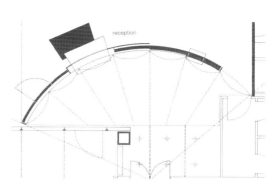

Headquarters, Piccadilly

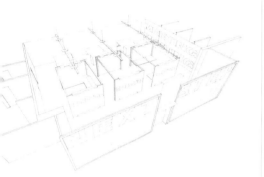

Next Step Guidance and Training Centre, Hayes

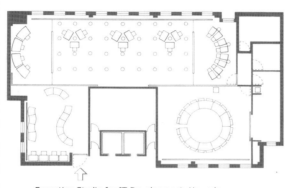

Executive Studio for IT Development, Hounslow

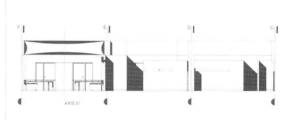

Business Development Centre, Park Royal

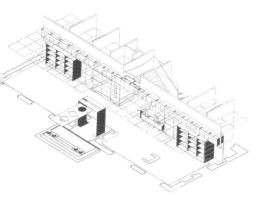

Community Opportunities Centre, Southall

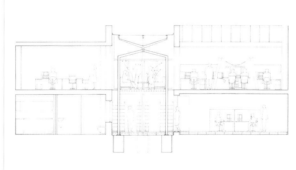

Film Viewing Suite and Film Library, Fitzroy Square

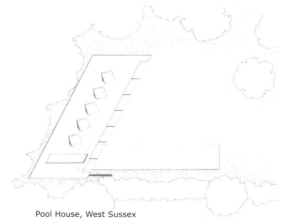

Pool House, West Sussex

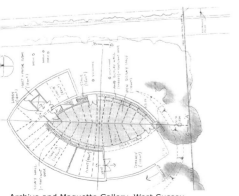

Archive and Maquette Gallery, West Sussex

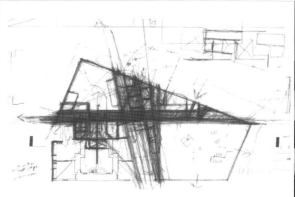

Mixed Use Gateway Building, King's Cross Central

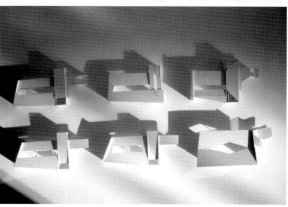

Study Centre, Exhibition Road

Biographies

After graduating from Duncan of Jordanstone College of Art, the University of Dundee, Craig Downie worked primarily for the offices of Lanchester and Lodge, Terry Farrell and Norman Foster before founding Studio Downie Architects in late 1993. For the earlier projects, Evian-les-Bains, Osaka and the Lakeside Retreat he worked with his wife, Laura Downie, who was responsible for many of the key models and hand drawings including the Lakeside Retreat perspective.

The completion of projects for both the Cass Sculpture Foundation and the West London TEC allowed the office to nurture a direction. In 1994 he presented three pavilions to the Annual Conference of the Royal Incorporation of Architects in Scotland and in 1995 was one of six architects chosen for RIBA Exhibition, *Emerging Architects in the UK,* held in Tokyo.

In 1995 and 1998 he was chosen for two prestigious projects. The first was the Parker Library project for Corpus Christi College, Cambridge, which he worked on for three years, before its postponement. The second, the new study centre for the Royal Geographical Society, was completed in 2004 and won the Judges' Special Award for a particularly inspirational building at the British Construction Industry Awards in 2005.

In 1998 and 2001, his work was included in The Architecture Foundation's publication, *New Architects: A Guide to Britain's Best Young Architectural Practices*.

He has taught at the Architectural Association in London, has been a visiting critic at the UK Universities of Liverpool, Plymouth and Oxford Brookes and is also a RIBA competitions advisor. With the development of the practice he became more focused on the design concept and development of the projects and several staff became key project architects and associates of the office.

In 1994, Andrew Jackson, a graduate of Duncan of Jordanstone College of Art, joined the practice, working on several projects including the Cass Sculpture Foundation. He was project architect for Next Step Acton, the Opportunities Centre, Southall, St. James' Square, the Institute of Contemporary Arts and the Royal Geographical Society.

In 1996, David Hanna, a graduate of Oxford Brookes University and The Bartlett School of Architecture, became part of the team, working on the Institute of Contemporary Arts, Corpus Christi College, Cambridge and the Royal Geographical Society. From 2003, he became project architect in charge of the completion of the Royal Geographical Society, project architect for the Cass Sculpture Foundation Centre completed in 2005 and worked with Craig Downie on St. Thomas' Hospital and King's Cross Central. He originally trained as a professional classical musician, graduating from the Royal College of Music, before turning to architecture. His interests include restoring classic cars and the restoration of antique stringed musical instruments.

In 1997 Christopher Binsted, a graduate of De Montfort University and The University of Westminster, joined Studio Downie and worked on Corpus Christi College, Cambridge, the Institute of Contemporary Arts, The Image Bank and the Royal Geographical Society. From 2000 he was project architect for the Ondaatje Theatre, several Royal Park cafés, the offices of Inspired Movies and the library for the Royal College of Surgeons of England and is currently working with Craig Downie on the Lyme Regis Museum. His interests include poetry, social studies and the psychological impact of colour. He is also a RIBA Councillor.

Project timeline

1993

Shortlisted competition entry for the lakeside housing and commercial masterplan for Evian-les-bains

Design studies for a Lakeside Retreat, California

Gallery and visitor's pavilion for the Cass Sculpture Foundation, The Goodwood Estate, West Sussex

Design studies for a meditation retreat for a recording studio, Little Wymondley, Hertfordshire

1994

Next Step Guidance and Training Centre for West London TEC, Acton Town, London

Business development centre for the Park Royal Partnership, Park Royal, London

Business Link for business development for West London TEC, Hounslow, London

UK headquarters for CDC Investment Management, The Caisse des Dépôts Group, Piccadilly, London

Special needs apartments for the Sanctuary Housing Association, Beaconsfield Road, London

1995

Design studies for a new canal side 15,000-square-foot office development for the British Waterways Board, Park Royal, London

Design studies for new beachside housing development, Goa, India

Community Opportunities Centre for West London TEC, Southall Town Hall, Southall, London

Next Step Guidance and Training Centre for West London TEC, Hayes, London

Mobile presentation and exhibition unit for SLI – Concord Lighting Truck, Europe

1996

Shortlisted competition entry for the visitor education centre for Chase Nature Reserve and Eastbrookend Country Park, Barking & Dagenham, London

Design studies for an art gallery and private residence extension to a listed building, Beuvron-en-Auge, Normandy

Private house refurbishment and extension, Halesworth, Suffolk

Interior design and wayfinding studies for Heathrow, Terminal 2, London

Library, archives and visitors' exhibition space for Corpus Christi College, Cambridge

Design studies for a construction skills training workshop for the London Borough of Hounslow, Feltham De Broome Centre, London

1997

Urban design masterplan studies for riverside retail development, for the London Borough of Twickenham, Twickenham, London

Landscape design for a city centre public space for the Human Rights Sculpture, Sheffield

New business and conference centre for West London TEC, West London Centre, London

Space planning of 50,000-square-foot headquarters building for 250 staff for West London TEC, West London Centre, London

Executive Studio for IT Development for West London TEC, Hounslow, London

Office headquarters building for BAA-Lynton, St. James's Square, London

Film viewing suite, film library and offices for The Image Bank, Fitzroy Square, London

Interior design for three high specification apartments for BAA-Lynton, Headfort Place, London

1998

Design studies for a demountable Next Step/Opportunities Centre for West London TEC, Twickenham, London

Design studies for a rooftop art gallery within Docklands warehouse for Bow Arts, London

Design studies for two 6000-square-foot country houses, Fulmer, Buckinghamshire

Office upgrade and new boardroom facilities for headquarters building for BAA-Lynton, Albany House, London

Business training centre interactive boardroom table for KPMG / Microsoft, Reading

Marketing exhibition display for the Cass Sculpture Foundation at the Building Design Centre

Exhibition, library, archives and education centre for the Royal Geographical Society (IBG), Exhibition Road, London

1999

Design studies for an archive, maquette gallery and offices for the Cass Sculpture Foundation, The Goodwood Estate, West Sussex

Design studies for refurbishment and remodelling of 50,000-square-foot existing building to offices/hotel for BAA-Lynton, Eaton House, Hounslow

Design studies for a new 6000-square-foot private house, Mill Hill, London

Gallery, media centre and restaurant, Institute of Contemporary Arts, The Mall, London

Pool house, Binderton, West Sussex

2000

House refurbishment and extension, Muswell Hill, London

Design studies for a house refurbishment and garden studio, Twickenham, London

Interior upgrade for The Ondaatje Theatre, Royal Geographical Society (IBG), Exhibition Road, London

Design studies including foyer and toilet improvement proposals for The Barbican Centre, London

Two 3000-square-foot mews houses, St Stephen's Mews, London

2001

Design studies for access improvements for The Architectural Association, London

2002

Restaurant, café and bar area for the Institute of Contemporary Arts, The Mall, London

Design study for a contemporary extension to Victorian mansion, Tunbridge Wells, Kent

Design studies for interior upgrade for Kenwood House, Hampstead Heath, London

Restaurant and kitchen interior upgrade for The Pavilion Tea House, Greenwich Park, London

2003

Shortlisted competition entry for the visitor pavilion and exhibition space for The Florence Nightingale Museum

Shortlisted competition entry for a new undergraduate library and study centre for Corpus Christi College, Cambridge

Shortlisted competition entry for the archives and study centre for National Maritime Museum

Competition entry for a 9/11 memorial, Pentagon, Washington DC

Shortlisted competition entry for the Royal Ballet School, White Lodge, Richmond-upon-Thames

Shortlisted competition entry for a conservation centre, staff offices and facilities for the British Library Centre For Conservation, St. Pancras, London

Design studies for centralised community facilities, Fieldway Multimedia Centre, Croydon, London

Foundation centre, gallery, library and archives for the Cass Sculpture Foundation, The Goodwood Estate, West Sussex

Infrastructure and public facilities design study for New Addington Shopping Parade, Croydon, London

Restaurant interior upgrade for The Dell, Hyde Park, London

2004

Design studies for a parkland masterplan with new healthy living and community centre, Canvey Island

Archives, gallery and education centre for the Philpot Lyme Regis Museum, Lyme Regis, Dorset

Assessor for design proposals for three large housing estates, Tower Hamlets, London

Post production headquarters for Inspired Movies, Clipstone Street, London

3500-square-foot private house, Muswell Hill, London

Library and study centre interior upgrade for the Royal College Of Surgeons Of England, Lincolns Inns Field, London

Wayfinding and interior design studies to enhance users' experience of public areas for Guys' And St. Thomas' NHS Trust, St. Thomas' Hospital, London

2005

Mixed use gateway building for Argent Estates Ltd., King's Cross Central, London

New art supplies warehouse for Cass Art, Islington, London

Private mews house refurbishment, Weymouth Mews, London

Selected bibliography

Periodicals

Lakeside House

Welsh, John. *Building Design*, 20 November 1992, No. 1103, p. 18, 'Marine Life'.

Gallery and Visitor Pavilion, Cass Sculpture Foundation

Architecture Interieure Crée, August/September 1996, pp. 90–91, 'Culture 2001: La Galerie au Fond des Bois'.

Dawson, Susan. *The Architects' Journal*, 28 September 1995, Vol. 202 No. 12, pp. 47–49, 'Pavilion of Sculpted Simplicity'.

Finch, Paul. *The Architects' Journal*, 2 May 1996, Vol. 203 No. 17, p. 31, 'Economy of means'.

Hors-Série: Séquences Bois Aménagements Intérieurs, September 1996, pp. 16–18, 'Activités & Commerces, Galerie en Angleterre'.

Hyde, Roger. *The Arup Journal*, 1/1996, pp. 18–19, 'Hat Hill Sculpture Foundation'.

Kemp, Candy. *Portfolio*, No. 6, p. 66, 'Twenty acres of woodland walks and glades provide an idyllic setting for forty important and innovative works by British Sculptors'.

Lloyd Morgan, Conway. *World Architecture*, No. 34, pp. 110–113, 'Computing: Wireframe in the Woods'.

Nikkei Architecture, 28 August 1995, No. 529.

Sharp, Dennis. *The Architects' Journal*, 20 October 1994, p. 12, 'Young British architects score a hit in Japan'.

Slessor, Catherine. *Architectural Review,* August 1995, No. 1182, pp. 65–67, 'Temple of the Arts'.

Stungo, Naomi. *RIBA Journal*, November 1994, Vol. 101 No. 11, pp. 38–43, 'Down to the Woods'.

Stungo, Naomi. *The Independent,* 14 December 1994, No. 2544, p. 27, 'A Breath of Californian Air'.

West London Training & Enterprise Council Interiors

Field, Marcus. *The Architects' Journal*, 25 April 1996, Vol. 203 No.16, pp. 42–45, 'Looking the Business'.

Finch, Paul. *The Architects' Journal*, 16 January 1997, Vol. 205 No. 2, p. 32, 'Work in Progress 2: Studio Downie West London Centre, Business Centre'.

McGuire, Penny. *Architectural Review*, April 1997, No. 1202, p. 92, 'Social Service'.

Stungo, Naomi. *RIBA Interiors*, May 1996, Vol. 103 No. 5, pp. 22–25, 'Golden Opportunity'.

CDC Investment Management UK Headquarters

Field, Marcus. *The Architects' Journal*, 25 April 1996, Vol. 203 No.16, pp. 42–45, 'Looking the Business'.

Human Rights Sculpture, Sheffield

Powell, Kenneth. *The Architects' Journal*, 22 October 1998, Vol. 208 No.15, p. 39, 'Sheffield Special: Current Projects'.

Image Bank

Dawson, Susan. *The Architects' Journal*, 06/13 August 1998, Vol. 208 No. 6, pp. 3, 39–41, 'Radical Intervention'.

Ondaatje Theatre

Baillieu, Amanda. *RIBA Interiors,* April 2002, pp. 28–30, 'Travel Story'.

The Courier and Advertiser, 15 March 2002, p. 8, 'Design for Success'.

Royal Geographical Society

Bell, Jonathan. *FX*, May 2001, No. 86, pp. 88–92, 'Transcending Tradition'.

Gardner, Rita. *Geographical*, June 2004, pp. 24–28, 'Unlocking the Archives'.

Henderson, Mark. *The Times*, 3 June 2004, p. 13, 'Archive Offers Key To World Of Discovery'.

Kennedy, Maev. *The Guardian*, 19 February 2002, p. 6, '£6m Plan To Show Geographical Society Archives'.

Melvin, Jeremy. *RIBA Journal,* September 2004, No. 111/9, pp. 26–32, 'Discovery Channel'.

Murray, Peter. *Royal Academy of Arts Magazine,* Autumn 2005, No. 88, p. 32, 'Open Sesame'.

Ralph-Knight, Lynda. *Design Week*, 10 June 04, Vol. 19 No. 24, p. 6, 'The Royal Geographical Society … '.

Pearman, Hugh. *Sunday Times Culture Magazine*, 06 June 2004, pp. 18–19, 'Sunken Treasures'.

Slessor, Catherine. *Architectural Review*, September 2004, Vol. 216 No. 1291, pp. 70–73, 'Geography Lesson'.

Stevenson, Agnes. *The Herald Magazine,* 13 November 2004, pp. 32–33, 'The Vault Lines Redrawn'.

Wilce, Hilary. *Times Education Supplement,* 28 May 2004, p. 18, 'Records of an Empire'.

Institute of Contemporary Arts

Li, Miranda. *Space: Night Out*, March 2006, pp. 202–207, 'The Institute of Contemporary Arts'.

Lister, David. *The Independent*, 18 March 2000, p. 9, 'ICA Defies Queen With Jazzy New Look'.

King's Cross Central

Bennett, Ellen. *Building Design,* 18 March 2005, p. 3, 'New Blood for King's Cross'.

Foundation Centre

Amadei, Gianluca. *Art and Architecture Journal*, Summer 2006, No. 66, pp. 28–31, 'Architecture: Studio Downie'.

Mead, Andrew. *The Architects' Journal*, 20 April 2006, Vol. 223 No. 15, pp. 31–45, 'Building Study'.

Rose, Steve. *G2* (*The Guardian* supplement), 15 May 2006, pp. 20–21, 'Can't see the Wood for the Trees'.

Young, Eleanor. *RIBA Journal*, June 2006, No. 113/6, pp. 56–60, 'Fruit of the Forest'.

Books

1000 Architects, The Images Publishing Group, Melbourne, 2004

Architects of the New Millennium, The Images Publishing Group, Melbourne, 2000

Bahamón, Alejandro, *The Magic of Tents: Transforming Space*, Harper Design International/LOFT Publications, New York 2004

Cloarec, Marion and Frédéric Mialet, *Séquences Bois: de vêture en structure, le bois, un matériau moderne, 100 réalisations pour témoigner*, CNDB/Editions du layer, Paris, 1997.

Details in Architecture Vol. 1 (1999)*, Vol. 5* (2004)*, Vol. 6* (2005), The Images Publishing Group, Melbourne

Elliot, Ann, *Sculpture at Goodwood*, Sculpture at Goodwood, Goodwood, 1995 & 2000

Frost, Malcolm, *Graphic Design for Architects*, The Images Publishing Group, Melbourne, 2002

Interior Spaces of Europe Vol 2, The Images Publishing Group, Melbourne, 1999

International Architecture Yearbook No. 3 (1997) and *International Architecture Yearbook No. 4* (1997), The Images Publishing Group, Melbourne

Micheli, Simone, *OFX Architettura Design Contract International Guide*, Design Diffusion Edizioni, Milan, 2000

New Architects: A guide to Britain's best young architectural practices, The Architectural Foundation, Booth Clibborn Editions, London 1998

New Architects 2: A guide to Britain's best young architectural practices, The Architectural Foundation, Merrell, London 2001

New Public Art, City of Westminster, London 2005

Office Spaces Vol 1, The Images Publishing Group, Melbourne 2003

Pearman, Hugh, *Contemporary World Architecture*, Phaidon, London, 1998

Prelorenzo, Claude et al, *La Ville au Bord de l'Eau: Une Lecture Thématique d'Europan 2*, Editions Parenthèses, Marseille, 1993

Sculpture at Goodwood: a vision for twenty-first century British sculpture, Sculpture at Goodwood, Goodwood, 2002

Social Spaces of the World Vol 1 (2000) & *Social Spaces of the World Vol 2* (2003), The Images Publishing Group, Melbourne

Turner, Janet, *Designing With Light – Public Spaces Lighting Solutions for Exhibitions, Museums and Historic Spaces*, Rotovision, Crans-prés-Cèligny, Switzerland, 1998

Zampi, Giuliano and Conway Lloyd Morgan, *Virtual Architecture*, Batsford, London, 1995

Lectures

1993 Royal Incorporation of Architects in Scotland Conference, Perth

1994 Architecture Institute of Japan, Tokyo

1996 University of East London

1996, 1997, 1998 Architectural Association, London

1997–1998 University of Aberdeen, University of Cardiff, University of Brighton

2000 The Design School

2002 Taking Shape, Hampshire Sculpture Trust, Winchester

2004, 2005 Central St. Martins College of Art, London

2004 Bath University

2005 Dundee Institute of Architects

2005 Outside/In, Society of Garden Designers Conference, Imperial College, London

2005 GLC Architecture Club

2005 Studio Culture 3 Conference, Royal College of Art, London

Exhibitions

La Maison d'Architecture, Paris and French Regions, Séquences Bois Aménagements Intérieurs, Ministère de la Culture, Paris, 1996

Recreation By Design, Royal Institute of British Architects, London, June 2003

Architectural Institute of Japan, Tokyo, 1994

How Did They Do That, Gallery 1 Royal Institute of British Architects, London, August 1996

Evian-les-bains Masterplan, Geneva and Evian-les-bains, 1993

Achievements and awards

1993 Studio Downie Architects established.

1993 Appointed Foundation Architect for the Cass Sculpture Foundation.

1993 Approved consultant for the London Docklands Development Corporation.

1993 Urban design project shortlisted by Dominique Perrault and Cedric Price and exhibited in Geneva and Evian-les-Bains, France.

1994 Appointed architects for a series of 12 projects for the West London Training & Enterprise Council.

1994 Appointed design advisors for BAA Heathrow Airport Limited (HAL).

1994 National winner of Design Business Association (DBA) Design Effectiveness Award in the office and commercial sector for the West London TEC, Next Step, Acton Town.

1994 Gallery and visitor's pavilion completed for the Cass Sculpture Foundation and shortlisted for British Construction Industry Awards.

1994 One of six practices chosen for the RIBA exhibition and seminar series, 'Emerging Architecture in the UK: Sense of Place, Sense of Age' chaired by Dr. Kisho Kurokawa, curated by Professor Dennis Sharp at the Architectural Institute of Japan, Tokyo.

1995 Commendation EMAP Architecture Tomorrow Awards for the gallery and visitor's pavilion for the Cass Sculpture Foundation.

1996 Chosen from an invited shortlist for The Parker Library and Archives for Corpus Christi College, Cambridge.

1996 Solo exhibition held at the RIBA Gallery 1 for the gallery and visitor's pavilion for the Cass Sculpture Foundation.

1997 Urban design advisor for Twickenham riverside site.

1998 and 2001 Included in the Architecture Foundation, London publication *New Architects: A Guide To Britain's Best Young Architectural Practices*.

1998 Chosen for the new exhibition, library, archives and education centre for the Royal Geographical Society (IBG), London.

2001 Chosen from an invited shortlist for the The Ondaatje Theatre, Royal Geographical Society (IBG), London.

2004 Chosen from an invited shortlist for the Royal College of Surgeons of England Library.

2004 Chosen from an invited shortlist for the new galleries and education centre for the Philpot Lyme Regis Museum.

2004 Study centre for the Royal Geographical Society (IBG) completed.

2005 Commissioned by Argent Estates Ltd. for a new mixed-use building as part of the King's Cross Central development.

2005 Runner-up for the Brick Awards for the Royal Geographical Society (IBG).

2005 Shortlisted for the Civic Trust Awards for the Royal Geographical Society (IBG).

2005 Shortlisted for the Copper Awards for the Royal Geographical Society (IBG).

2005 Winner of an RIBA Commendation for Conservation for the Royal Geographical Society (IBG).

2005 Winner of the Judges' Special Award for a particularly inspirational building from the British Construction Industry (BCI) Awards for the Study Centre, Royal Geographical Society (IBG).

2005 Foundation Centre, Cass Sculpture Foundation completed.

Photography/image credits

All images/photographs not noted below: Studio Downie Architects

Opposite title page: Peter Cook
Projects divider (p. 10): Morley von Sternberg
Front cover image of Cass Sculpture Foundation: Katsuhisa Kida
Back cover image of Cass Sculpture Foundation: Peter Cook

Gallery and Visitors' Pavilion, Cass Sculpture Foundation

Peter Cook: pp. 12, 14, 15 (bottom), 16 (bottom), 17 (centre), 18, 20 (top left, bottom left), 20–23
Katsuhisa Kida: pp. 15 (top), 16 (middle), 19, 17 (top right)

Guidance, training and business development centres, West London TEC

Peter Cook: pp. 32, 34–37, 40–41
Chris Gascoigne: pp. 38–39

UK Headquarters for The Caisse des Dépôts Group

All photography: Peter Cook

Community Opportunities Centre, West London TEC

All photography: Peter Cook

Office Headquarters Building, BAA-Lynton

All photography: Chris Gascoigne

Executive Studio for IT Development, West London TEC

All photography: Chris Gascoigne

Film Viewing Suite, Film Library and Offices, The Image Bank

All photography: Peter MacKinven

Gallery, Media Centre and Restaurant, Institute of Contemporary Arts (ICA)

All photography: James Morris

Ondaatje Theatre, Royal Geographical Society

All photography: James Morris

Study Centre, Royal Geographical Society

Morley von Sternberg: pp. 78, 88–91 (top), 95
James Morris: pp. 79–87, 91 (bottom), 92–94

Library and Study Centre, Royal College of Surgeons of England

From the archives of the Royal College of Surgeons of England: p. 97 (bottom)

Foundation Centre, Cass Sculpture Foundation

All photography: Peter Cook

City Square Landmark, Osaka, Japan